A Change of Heart

English Architecture Since the War
a policy for protection

Royal Commission on the Historical Monuments of England
English Heritage

Published by the Royal Commission on the Historical Monuments of England,
Fortress House, 23 Savile Row, London W1X 2JQ

© Royal Commission on the Historical Monuments of England and English Heritage 1992
First published 1992

ISBN 1 873592 12 4

British Library Cataloguing in Publication Data
A CIP catalogue record for this book is available from the British Library

Printed in Great Britain by Pegasus Print and Display Ltd,
10 Osier Way, Mitcham, Surrey CR4 4NF

Foreword

English Heritage was set up to advance our understanding and care of historic buildings, and the Royal Commission on the Historical Monuments of England to survey and record them. Our complementary aims are brought together in this book, launched to coincide with a major exhibition held at the Royal College of Art in July and August 1992. It celebrates the wealth and range of fine architecture produced in England since the Second World War, and addresses the thorny problem of how best to preserve it.

Our growing appreciation and understanding of Victorian, Edwardian and inter-war architecture – once often derided and despised – have led to a general acceptance that the best should be protected. No such consensus yet exists on post-war buildings. Whilst a very small number – twenty-nine to date – have been listed, ranging from the traditional Bracken House of the 1950s to the innovative Willis Faber Building of 1975, many more recommendations for listing made to Ministers by English Heritage have been rejected.

People still react passionately to post-war architecture. Many are hostile because of the failures that stick in the mind. But much is excellent and exciting, and it is possible now to assess both contemporary and subsequent criticism and the buildings themselves, especially those down to the late 1970s, with cool detachment. Both our Commissions are committed to broadening the public debate and, to this end, English Heritage is engaged in a research programme designed to define the criteria and provide guidelines for the listing of post-war buildings which will be presented for government approval. This will lead to a separate publication in due course.

We believe a change of heart is overdue. This book and the exhibition it accompanies will launch the great debate about the best ways to protect the best architecture of the post-war era.

Park of Monmouth

Jocelyn Stevens

We would like here to express our appreciation to the Obayashi Corporation and Pearson plc (the previous and current owners of Bracken House, England's first post-war listed building) for their financial support for the exhibition.

Pavilion Restaurant, Oxford Street, London. Interior decoration designed by Angus McBean, 1951. Destroyed 1987. Photograph: RCHME

A Change of Heart

Send to us power and light ...

... look shining at

New styles of architecture, a change of heart.

W H Auden

The past is catching up with us. Once, the listing of buildings was confined to buildings that were especially beautiful or old. But in every Western country, as we learn more about our history and culture, we value the recent past also and cherish the best of its architecture.

Not so long ago, Victorian buildings were derided. The architecture of the two inter-war decades has excited enthusiasts only in the past few years. Now, it is the British architecture of the years after the Second World War that is being rediscovered.

There is much more to this than fashion. Buildings grow out of date ever more quickly; their life cycles have become unpredictable. Much recent architecture designed for a long life is now obsolescent. In cities,

Bracken House, Cannon Street, City of London, a corner tower. Richardson and Houfe, architects, 1955–9. Listed Grade II in 1987. Photograph: RCHME*

1

the commercial pressure to throw buildings away and replace them intensifies. At the same time many lightly constructed modern buildings, once expected to last only for a generation, are having to soldier on, reconditioned at best. When the future of a building comes into question, perhaps because it has become uneconomic, perhaps because it needs major overhaul, decisions have to be made. A growing number of the most original works of modern British architecture have come under the shadow of demolition or alteration in the past few years. A few have disappeared. If the best of these buildings are to be safeguarded for posterity, the reassessment of our post-war architectural heritage cannot wait.

Yet there are great difficulties. Our view of post-war architecture has been tainted by a sense of failure, incomprehension and dislike. Wrongly, it is identified with the harsher styles, materials and methods of the Modern Movement alone, obdurately unloved in England outside the building professions. It is associated still with arrogant city-planning, mistaken housing policies and a false utopianism.

But as the thirty years from the end of the Second World War to the oil-price crisis of the mid 1970s dissolve into history, things begin to look different. Far from being uniform and monotonous in character, we

Newton Building, Nottingham (formerly Trent) Polytechnic. T Cecil Howitt, architect, 1956–8.
Photograph: RCHME

3

start to realise that post-war architecture was of unsuspected, often bewildering variety, richness and inventiveness. We can once more value the courage and drive of post-war reconstruction and now acknowledge what was good as well as what was bad in the period's unprecedented social building programmes.

There was enormous pent-up energy after 1945. Six years of hostilities had reduced our cities to a mess, our towns to scruffiness and dinginess. Behind that lay the memory of pervasive depression during the 1930s and the century-old legacy of the Industrial Revolution: social inequalities tolerated too long, slum housing, filth in the workplace, soot in the streets and a shabby urban environment without space, greenness, order or variety of scale.

During the war, soldiers and citizens alike had come to accept the need for national goals and national programmes. With a final, supreme effort of organisation, their discipline and energy were now to be harnessed to peaceful ends and a fresh social start. A great experiment was presaged, in which architecture – for the first time in British history – would play a heroic role. Architects and planners were to take the technical lead in directing the changes so ardently sought.

Town Square, Stevenage, Hertfordshire. Stevenage Development Corporation, architects and planners, 1956–8.
Photograph: RCHME

Younger men and women were inspired by the radicalism of the Modern Movement, which suited the national mood. Architectural modernism had been toyed with in 1930s Britain, most often as a slick style suitable for cinemas, roadhouses, resort hotels, pavilions and yacht clubs, zoo buildings or the occasional flat-roofed home for progressive-thinking people. Post-war modernism was to be something more fundamental and embracing – an approach to life, not just to style. The apostles of modernism claimed that science and art could be harnessed together to offer a quality of architecture that would, impartially, transform everyone's lives.

If this was to be achieved, the country would have to think big. Old cities needed to be fundamentally overhauled, complete new towns built, housing estates laid out on fresh principles, thousands of child-centred schools and dozens of universities constructed to cope with a growing population. Building production itself was to be revolutionised. It was a programme of awesome ambition, adopted in the teeth of national economic difficulties that often delayed and sometimes threatened to derail the whole experiment. In the end it ground gradually to a halt. Little by little, from the 'Cripps cuts' imposed by the Labour Government in 1949 down to the oil-price inflation of 1973, the idealism of the immediate post-war years ebbed away.

St George's Church,
Stevenage, Hertfordshire.
Seely and Paget, architects,
1956–60.
Photograph: RCHME

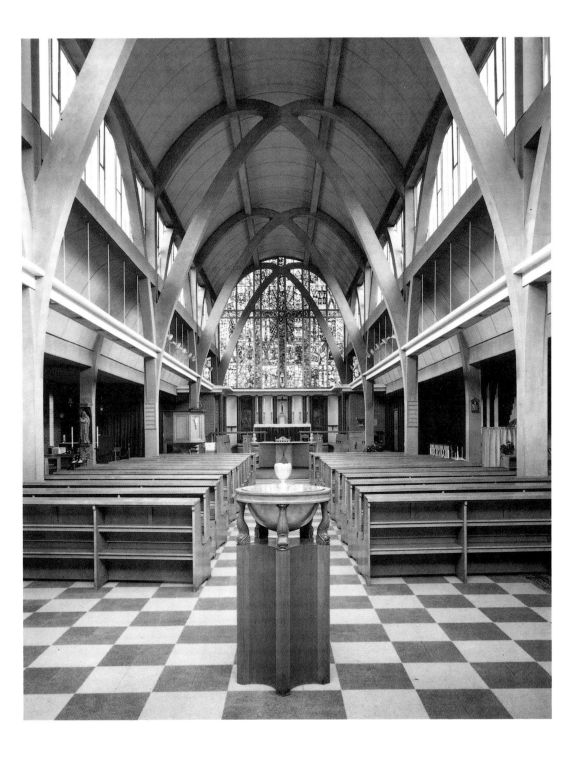

It has become easy to spot the mistakes of the post-war visionaries. They overestimated untried technology and its ability to change our lives for the better. They underestimated the power of habit and of familiarity in shaping places that make us happy. In their haste to improve everyone's lot, they tried to build too much too fast and too cheaply. Scarce resources were shared out equally among many projects, to the impoverishment of most of them; in architecture, as in everything else, you get only what you pay for. Nor did the post-war architects allow for the chronic individualism of the British, who by and large do not like austere uniformity imposed upon them, especially in their homes. Rarely did they manage to make contact with those who were to use and live in their buildings. Preoccupied as they were with the notion of an avant-garde in architecture, they were surprised when their efforts were spurned as incomprehensible, impractical or downright ugly.

But against what went wrong there needs to be set what went right – too often forgotten now, because so easily taken for granted. Our cities are far less filthy and monotonous than they were fifty years ago. Nineteen New Towns have been built to coherent plans and with a quiet purpose and decency that have impressed urbanists the world over. Most people live, learn and work in places that have an environment and facilities they could hardly have dreamt of in 1945. Their eyes, too, have

Runcorn–Widnes Transporter Bridge. Mott, Hay and Anderson, engineers, 1956–61. Listed Grade II in 1988. Photograph: RCHME

9

been opened to fresher, less insular ways of going about art, architecture and design. The changes to British architecture wrought by the post-war modernists can only be compared in profundity to those that happened a hundred years before, when Pugin and his Gothic principles threw over the slack eclecticism of the Regency. They belong to our history, and we need to come to terms with them. They gave birth, too, to some new places and many new buildings in which we have every reason to take pride today.

We have been slow to digest the range of the post-war architectural heritage. Bemused by modernism in its most forceful guise, when we think of post-war architecture we conjure up tall, concrete-mullioned or curtain-walled structures slapped down in the middle of cities. There are plenty of such buildings, of varying value. But they represent the whole of the post-war years no better than, say, an iron-framed warehouse should stand for everything built between 1800 and 1830 – a period of equal architectural and technical turmoil. Tower blocks tell us nothing about the dogged continuity of traditionalism, about the fresh ways in which painting, sculpture and the crafts were brought to bear upon buildings, or about the renaissance of British civil engineering design – all vital themes in the post-war saga.

St Paul's Church, Bow Common, London. Maguire and Murray, architects, 1957–8. Listed Grade II in 1988.*
Photograph: English Heritage

The types of building that have fallen into disrepute also offer a misleading image of modernism, an architectural chameleon with many modes of expression. Modernism is impossible to define succinctly. But the consistent strands in it are these: the urge for architecture to free itself from the old historical styles; to take the function that buildings are to perform as the first cue to their planning and appearance; to design buildings from the interior outwards; and to offer a sense of liberal space and freedom, inside and out, in lieu of trivial architectural detail.

Three strands in British modern architecture can be identified: the modernism of method, the modernism of style and the modernism of good manners. First off the mark after the war is the modernism of method. It is the most radical form of modernism, though its buildings do not always look the most revolutionary. It is the modernism of Gropius and the Dessau Bauhaus, adopted by the architects seriously committed to the great social building programmes – new towns, new housing, new schools. Many of them worked anonymously for local or central government departments or development corporations, to whom these great programmes were largely entrusted. The modernism of method implies teamwork. It means integrating the design of buildings with their production and developing that design systematically from one project to the next. Anything and everything to do with a building

Bankside Power Station, Southwark, London. Architect Sir Giles Gilbert Scott, with Mott, Hay and Anderson, engineers, 1957–60. Photograph: English Heritage

13

undergoes scrutiny: its structure, setting, materials, services, distribution of costs, means of production and life cycle.

The great success of the modernism of method was in school building. To ensure that everyone had access to the flood of ideas entering the debate about education and building in the wake of the Butler Education Act of 1944, central government pressed teams of local authority architects to turn their backs upon individual display and build their schools in annual programmes, using a common method of construction. Many of the schools they built look so simple and modest that we might not care to call them architecture at all. Yet they were the fruit of intense development and the envy of architects and educationalists abroad.

The modernism of style is more readily understood. For most architects working in private practice, modernism meant an increasingly international conception of style. Since the Modern Movement had been slow off the mark in Britain, they looked outwards for inspiration: first to older form-givers like Le Corbusier and Mies van der Rohe; later to younger heroes like Niemeyer in Brazil, Candela in Mexico, Kahn in America. Only at the end of the 1950s, when building licences were no longer needed and private commissions began to catch up with the

30A Hendon Lane, Finchley, London. Chamberlin, Powell and Bon, architects, 1958. Photograph: English Heritage

public-sector programmes, did modern styles in British architecture gain individuality or make much public impact. Before then, even the biggest modern buildings had been friendly, almost bland, in scale and material.

Then came the reaction: 'brutalism'. It was a movement far from confined to Britain, but one that found its name here and some of its ablest adherents among British architects who came of age around 1960. It was the counterpart of changes in international mood that followed upon Khrushchev's speech to the 20th Party Congress, upon Hungary and Suez. Liberalisation at home and decolonisation abroad were in the air. The angularity and muscularity of brutalism, its glorification of concrete textures and its sixties unruliness turn up in all sorts of structures, from the first motorway bridges to the anarchic South Bank. It has parallels with High Victorian architecture and with the baroque of Vanbrugh and Hawksmoor, both previous episodes of reaction against gentility. But it can be disciplined too, as it usually is in the new university buildings of the 1960s – the most prestigious building projects of the whole post-war era.

But perhaps the most typical British modernism was the modernism of good manners. When one looks with an impartial eye at the bulk of architecture in the thirty years after 1945, one is struck by its mildness,

The Queen's College, Oxford, Provost's Lodgings. Architect Raymond Erith, 1958–9. Photograph: English Heritage

its lack of dogma and rhetoric, its refusal to jettison tradition. Modernist features it certainly has, but it is a compromising modernism cribbing from Sweden, Denmark, Finland and Switzerland rather than Marseilles or Chicago. Behind it is the sense that the roots of the best modernism lie in Morris and the English Arts and Crafts tradition.

This gentlemanly modernism of compromise is that of the 'herbivores', as its adherents were sometimes contemptuously called. It is the modernism of the Festival of Britain, of Coventry Cathedral and, it should be acknowledged, of much of the best post-war housing. It is an architecture of brick and stone more than of concrete. It is as comfortable with the pitched roof as with the flat one. Like the modernism of the 1930s it firmly believes in fun (British architects seem to cheer up and give their best when given a place of entertainment to design). It is especially welcoming to the arts. Far from fading out, as might have been predicted, in the more mechanistic post-war world, the arts and the crafts enjoy a reconciliation with architecture. Between the wars, architectural ornament had become confined and trivialised. Now, the ornamental approach is abandoned. Instead, good artists are called upon to blazon their own idiom upon generous surfaces or spaces where their work can be properly viewed and appreciated. No decade is so rich in British public art as the 1950s, nor as yet so undervalued.

Coventry Cathedral,
St Michael and the Devil.
Sir Jacob Epstein, sculptor,
1958–9. Listed Grade I
in 1988.
Photograph: RCHME

Between the modernism of good manners and the architecture of the traditionalists – so sneered at in the 1950s, covered with such belated praise today – the gap is small. Pure architectural expression can rarely hide the purpose for which a building is built; at any given point in history such purposes have much in common. As the period recedes, we begin to see that traditional and anti-traditional solutions to post-war problems have many more shared features than differences.

The distinction, if any, is one of historical attitude. Many of the traditionalists still building in the 1950s and 1960s had enjoyed pre-war careers. They saw nothing wrong, and much wisdom, in going on with the old ways. On the technical side of things they now appear to have been vindicated. Many modernists were playing with techniques which were only half understood, as happens at any time of great changes in building technology (the great John Nash stands accused of the same fault). Costly mistakes were made, for which we are still paying.

On the other hand the modernists felt progress would never be made unless there was technical experimentation. In this they too were right. The internationally acclaimed British 'high-tech' architects of today could not play confidently with the pipes, servicing and cladding they take for granted had it not been for the trials and errors of modernism

Fylingdales Early Warning Station, North Yorkshire, the 'radomes'. Air Ministry Works Department, engineers, 1961–2.
Photograph: RCHME

in the 1950s and 1960s. The modernists too believed in history. Their history consisted not in historical styles to imitate – a cowardly procedure, they believed – but in the inspiration of the Crystal Palace, Victorian engineering and all previous building traditions of experiment and courage.

Now that we are eclectic in our architecture again, the post-war onslaught of the moderns against the ancients seems irrelevant – an attempt to reduce a healthy plurality to a single orthodoxy. But in the 1950s, despite the enthusiasm for reconstruction and a fresh start, British modernism was still a frail creature. Later, there was a period in the 1960s when it looked as if traditionalist British architecture might really disappear. It did not do so, because for several significant types of English building, modern solutions had never wholeheartedly appealed. The *Country Life* and *Ideal Home* readerships, for instance, had never been converted. As soon after the war as they could afford to, they went back to building and adding to their houses in neo-Georgian or neo-vernacular modes. Anglican churches likewise tended to be traditional, at any rate before the era of liturgical reform; and old skills and styles continued to be needed wherever old buildings were being restored or extended. This kept the traditionalists going through the bleakest years.

Elephant and Rhino House, London Zoo. Casson and Conder, architects, 1963–5. Photograph: RCHME

The solution to the quarrel is easy to see in retrospect. In the kind of building that has a short history or needs to be functional in design, modern styles have had no difficulty establishing themselves. Everyone can admire the great engineering structures dotted around the English landscape, when they are well designed. Bridges, power stations, factories and airports have a majesty of their own that has never required historical dress. Some other kinds of building, houses in particular, are so close to the British heart in tradition and sentiment that it has proved counter-productive to abjure history and continuity in their design. That leaves many types of building over which alternative styles of architecture – the plurality we again see as healthy – can still do battle. The modernist revolution has added hugely to the scope of our choices.

The process of protecting English post-war architecture is already under way. But it will take years to digest and classify the subject and to decide exactly which structures to safeguard and how. There are many practical problems. The listing system, for instance, works well for individual, separately conceived buildings. But a large proportion of the post-war architectural heritage consists of ensembles, estates and new communities. To control changes on complete housing estates, hundreds

University Centre, Cambridge, detail of staircase. Howell, Killick, Partridge and Amis, architects, 1965–7. Photograph: RCHME

of modest buildings would have to be listed. Conservation areas might be better solutions. Yet the protection they afford can be weak and fail to prevent unsightly changes. Another issue arises with the celebrated post-war primary schools, built in different places but with an ingenious common vocabulary of prefabricated components. Though among the foremost achievements of post-war English architecture, they were built with a comparatively short life in mind. They make sense only as a developing series. How many such structures should we aim to keep? In all these cases, we must find the form of protection that can preserve what is best, yet guide rather than prevent needed changes.

A start has been made with the 'thirty-year rule', operating since 1987. This allows the Government to list buildings that were started on the ground at least thirty years previously. If there is a serious threat of alteration or demolition and a building is deemed to be of especial merit, listing can occur after a building is ten years old. The thirty-year rule is not without difficulties, but it has the merit of enforcing perspective. The ups and downs of architectural reputations since 1945 warn us that we would be unwise to accept all that is currently fashionable in architecture as of permanent value. The first building to be listed under the new rule, in 1987, was Sir Albert Richardson's Bracken House in the City of London, a traditionalist design that was scoffed at or ignored at

Trellick Tower, Cheltenham Estate, Kensal Green, London. Ernö Goldfinger, architect, 1969–72.
Photograph: English Heritage

the time of its construction in the 1950s. We can make some good guesses about what will be eligible for listing in thirty years' time – two such buildings are illustrated in this booklet. But there are bound to be surprises; distance and dispassion are necessary.

Meanwhile, the task is to look again with an unprejudiced eye, to comprehend and to reassess the post-war years from today's ever-lengthening perspective. English Heritage is setting about the study of the chief building types of the period one by one. As this proceeds, we shall better understand its architecture in the light of what people wanted (or what it was thought they wanted) and what choices were available to them. Comparisons can then be made between buildings of the same kind, without the distraction of stylistic prejudice. We shall then be able to make a fairer selection of which buildings to protect. The Royal Commission is playing its part in the process by recording the architecture of the period. This booklet, and the exhibition that accompanies it, illustrate the first fruits of the two bodies' joint efforts.

Auden called in 1929 for moral conviction: 'New styles of architecture, a change of heart'. At that time, English culture seemed stale, lifeless and provincial. The energy of the 19th century had ebbed away upon the battlefields of the First World War. Britain seemed to

Orwell Bridge at Wherstead,
A45 Ipswich bypass.
Sir William Halcrow and
Partners, engineers, 1979–82.
Photograph: RCHME

soldier on in its inward-looking way, with its humdrum towns and cities, its sprawling suburbs and its placid, eroding countryside. The next decades were decades of conviction indeed – of grave destruction, great difficulties, but powerful experiment and creativity. It is not surprising that we have reacted against them and against the architecture of moral conviction. But we cannot do so for ever; indeed we have practically ceased to do so, for the period belongs to history. In our budding tolerance, even affection, for the challenging architecture of the post-war years, there are signs now of a further change of heart.

Andrew Saint

Schlumberger Research Building, Cambridge. Michael Hopkins and Partners, architects, 1983–5. Photograph: RCHME

Post-war Listed Buildings in England

Grade I
Royal Festival Hall, Lambeth, London. London County Council Architect's Department, 1948–51, 1963–5

Sir Bernard Lovell Telescope, Jodrell Bank, 1952–7

Coventry Cathedral. Sir Basil Spence, architect, 1958–62

Willis Faber Building, Ipswich. Foster Associates, architects, 1973–5

Grade II*
Stockwell Bus Garage, Lambeth, London. Adie, Button and Partners, architects, A E Beer, engineer, 1951–4

Congress House (TUC Headquarters), Camden, London. David Aberdeen, architect, 1953–7

Bracken House, City of London. Richardson and Houfe, architects, 1955–9

Sanderson House, Westminster, London. Slater, Uren and Moberly, architects, 1957–60

St Paul's, Tower Hamlets, London. Maguire and Murray, architects, 1957–8

Commonwealth Institute, Kensington, London. Robert Matthew, Johnson-Marshall and Partners, architects, 1960–2

Economist Building, Westminster, London. Alison and Peter Smithson, architects, 1962–4

Grade II
Burleigh School, Cheshunt, Hertfordshire. Hertfordshire County Council Architect's Department, 1946–8

Newbury Park Bus Station, Redbridge, London. Oliver Hill, architect, 1947–50

Three Standing Figures, Battersea Park, London. Henry Moore, sculptor, 1948–50

15–19 Aubrey Walk, Kensington, London. Raymond Erith, architect, 1951–2

Time-Life Building, Westminster, London. Michael Rosenauer, architect, with Hugh Casson, Misha Black and others, 1951–3

1 Dean Trench Street, Westminster, London. H S Goodhart-Rendel, architect, 1951–5

St Columba's, Pont Street, Chelsea, London. Sir Edward Maufe, architect, 1952–4

All Saints, Hanworth, London. N F Cachemaille-Day and Partners, architects, 1952–7

Hallfield School, Paddington, London. Drake and Lasdun, architects, 1953–4

St John's, Newbury, Berkshire. Stephen Dykes-Bower, architect, 1955–7

45–46 Albemarle Street, Westminster, London. Ernö Goldfinger, architect, 1955–7

The Pediment, Aynho, Northamptonshire. Raymond Erith, architect, 1956–7

Runcorn–Widnes Transporter Bridge. Mott, Hay and Anderson, engineers, 1956–61

20 Blackheath Park, Greenwich, London. Peter Moro, architect, 1957–8

Exeter University Chapel, Devon. Vincent Harris, architect, 1957–8

Cripps Hall, University of Nottingham. McMorran and Whitby, architects, 1957–9

The Cedar House, Bromley, London. Howell, Killick, Partridge and Amis, architects, 1958–60

Jack Straw's Castle, Hampstead, London. Raymond Erith, architect, 1962–4

Marco Polo Building, Queenstown Road, Battersea, London. Ian Pollard, architect-developer, 1987–8. Photograph: RCHME

Further Reading

There are few worthwhile books on British architecture for the period 1945 to 1975. The best source on the 1950s and 1960s remains the contemporary journals, especially the *Architectural Review*, particularly for the early 1950s, and *Architectural Design*, more weighted towards brutalism. The *Buildings of England* series, founded by Sir Nikolaus Pevsner in 1951, has from the first been notably strong on recent buildings; the actual coverage of each volume varies because of the widely different dates of first publication and of any subsequent revision.

General Works

Peter Kidson, Peter Murray and Paul Thompson, *A History of English Architecture*. Penguin, 1978

William J R Curtis, *Modern Architecture since 1900*. Phaidon, 1982

Boris Ford (ed), *The Cambridge Guide to the Arts in Britain, vol 9: Since the Second World War*. Cambridge University Press, 1988

Contemporary Accounts

Trevor Dannatt, *Modern Architecture in Britain*. Batsford, 1959

Nicholas Taylor and Philip Booth, *Cambridge New Architecture*. Leonard Hill, 1964, 1965, 1970

Reyner Banham, *The New Brutalism*. Architectural Press, 1966

Anthony Jackson, *The Politics of Architecture*. Architectural Press, 1970

Reyner Banham, *Megastructure*. Thames and Hudson, 1976

Recent Specialised Works

Mary Banham and Bevis Hillier, *A Tonic to the Nation*. Thames and Hudson, 1976

Lionel Esher, *A Broken Wave*. Allen Lane, 1981

James Dunnett and Gavin Stamp, *Ernö Goldfinger*. Architectural Association, 1983

Lucy Archer, *Raymond Erith*. Cygnet Press, 1985

Andrew Saint, *Towards a Social Architecture*. Yale, 1987

35